Primary Sources of the Civil Rights Movement

Martin Luther King Jr. and Peaceful Protest

Kelly Spence

New York

Published in 2017 by Cavendish Square Publishing, LLC
243 5th Avenue, Suite 136, New York, NY 10016

First Edition

Website: cavendishsq.com

CPSIA Compliance Information: Batch #CS16CSQ

All websites were available and accurate when this book was sent to press.

Library of Congress Cataloging-in-Publication Data

Names: Spence, Kelly, author.
Title: Martin Luther King Jr. and peaceful protest / Kelly Spence.
Description: New York : Cavendish Square Publishing, 2016. | Series: Primary sources of the civil rights movement | Includes bibliographical references and index. | Description based on print version record and CIP data provided by publisher; resource not viewed.
Identifiers: LCCN 2016000362 (print) | LCCN 2015049738 (ebook) | ISBN 9781502618658 (ebook) | ISBN 9781502618641 (library bound)
Subjects: LCSH: King, Martin Luther, Jr., 1929-1968--Juvenile literature. | African Americans--Biography--Juvenile literature. | Civil rights workers--United States--Biography--Juvenile literature. | African Americans--Civil rights--History--20th century--Juvenile literature. | Civil rights movements--United States--History--20th century--Juvenile literature. | Nonviolence--United States--History--20th century--Juvenile literature.
Classification: LCC E185.97.K5 (print) | LCC E185.97.K5 S67 2016 (ebook) | DDC 323.092--dc23
LC record available at http://lccn.loc.gov/2016000362

Editorial Director: David McNamara
Editor: Fletcher Doyle
Copy Editor: Nathan Heidelberger
Art Director: Jeffrey Talbot
Designer: Amy Greenan
Production Assistant: Karol Szymczuk
Photo Research: J8 Media

The photographs in this book are used by permission and through the courtesy of: Dick DeMarsico, World Telegram staff photographer/Library of Congress/File:Martin Luther King Jr NYWTS.jpg/Wikimedia Commons, cover; Engraving by W. Roberts/File:EmancipationProclamation.jpg/Wikimedia Commons, 5; Jack Delano/PhotoQuest/Getty Images, 6; Yoshio Tomii/SuperStock/Getty Images, 9; AP Photo/AJC, 10; Larry Burrows/The LIFE Picture Collection/Getty Images, 12; Unknown/File:Salt March.jpg/Wikimedia Commons, 13; Michael Evans/New York Times Co./Getty Images, 15; © John Frost Newspapers/Alamy Stock Photo, 16; Universal History Archive/Getty Images, 19; Grey Villet/The LIFE Picture Collection/Getty Images, 20; AP Photo, 21; Background Map: 1961 Freedom Rides (New York): Associated Press News Feature/Library of Congress Geography & Map Division, 25; Michael Ochs Archives/Getty Images, 29; AFP/Getty Images, 30; AP Photo, 32; AP Photo/Larry Stoddard, 35; AFP/Getty Images, 36; Three Lions/Getty Images, 37; Hulton Archive/Getty Images, 39; Marion S. Trikosko, U.S. News & World Report Magazine/File:MLK and Malcolm X USNWR cropped.jpg/Wikimedia Commons, 40; AP Photo/Jack Thornell, 43; Joseph Louw/The LIFE Images Collection/Getty Images, 44; Declan Haun/Chicago History Museum/Getty Images, 46; AP Photo/Barry Thumma, 48; Universal History Archive/Getty Images, 49; Thomas S. England/Bloomberg via Getty Images, 51.

Printed in the United States of America

CONTENTS

INTRODUCTION

"Separate but Equal"

On January 1, 1863, President Abraham Lincoln freed millions of slaves living in the Confederate states by issuing the Emancipation Proclamation. This landmark action marked one of many steps that led to the civil rights movement of the 1950s and 1960s.

Amendments to the Constitution of the United States following the end of the Civil War in 1865 expanded the scope of the proclamation. They extended basic rights to black people, whether they were freed slaves or had never been a slave. The Thirteenth Amendment prohibited slavery and involuntary servitude "except as a punishment for crime whereof the party shall have been duly convicted." The Fourteenth Amendment asserted that no citizen would be denied "equal protection under the laws," while the Fifteenth Amendment stated that "the right of citizens of the United States to vote shall not be denied or abridged by the United States or by any State on account of race, color, or previous condition of servitude." In the North, these rights were

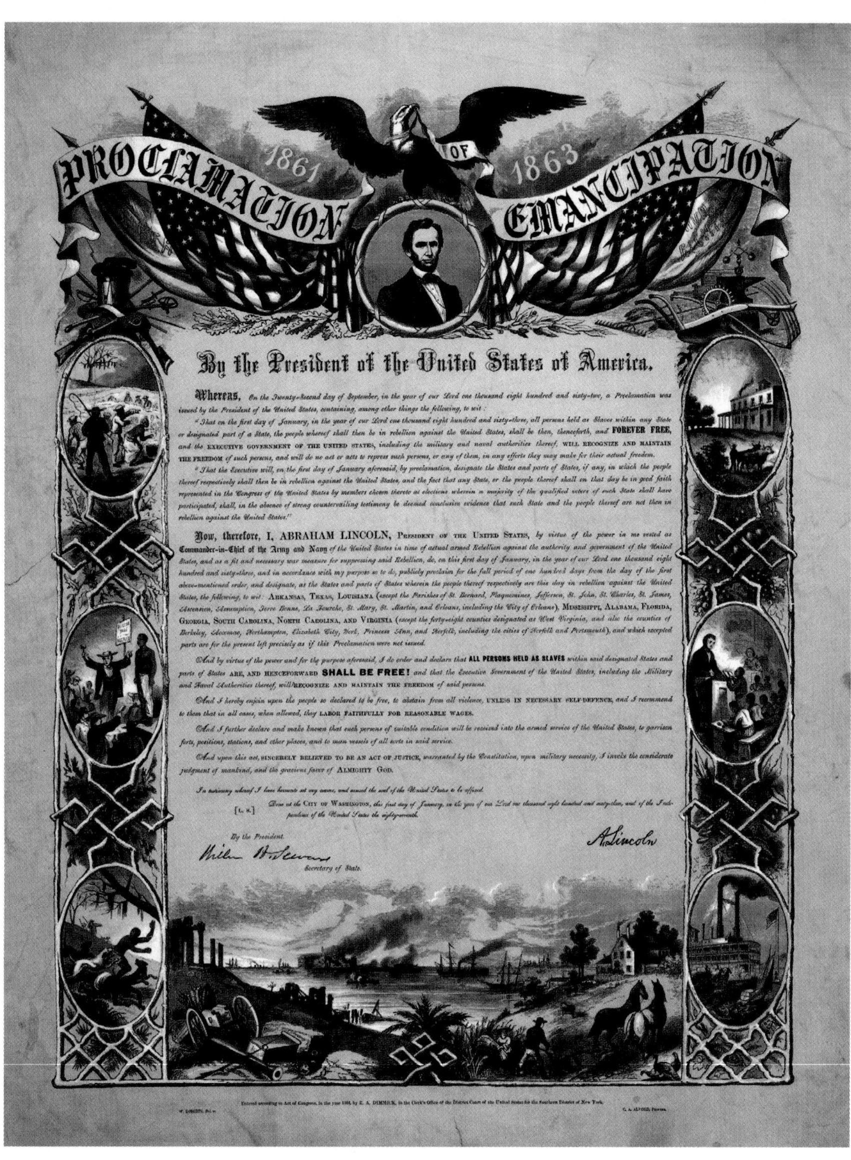

PROCLAMATION OF EMANCIPATION

1861 1863

By the President of the United States of America.

Whereas, On the Twenty-Second day of September, in the year of our Lord one thousand eight hundred and sixty-two, a Proclamation was issued by the President of the United States, containing, among other things the following, to wit:

"That on the first day of January, in the year of our Lord one thousand eight hundred and sixty-three, all persons held as Slaves within any State or designated part of a State, the people whereof shall then be in rebellion against the United States, shall be then, thenceforth, and **FOREVER FREE,** and the EXECUTIVE GOVERNMENT OF THE UNITED STATES, including the military and naval authorities thereof, WILL RECOGNIZE AND MAINTAIN THE FREEDOM of such persons, and will do no act or acts to repress such persons, or any of them, in any efforts they may make for their actual freedom.

"That the Executive will, on the first day of January aforesaid, by proclamation, designate the States and parts of States, if any, in which the people thereof respectively shall then be in rebellion against the United States, and the fact that any State, or the people thereof shall on that day be in good faith represented in the Congress of the United States by members chosen thereto at elections wherein a majority of the qualified voters of such State shall have participated, shall, in the absence of strong countervailing testimony be deemed conclusive evidence that such State and the people thereof are not then in rebellion against the United States."

Now, therefore, I, ABRAHAM LINCOLN, PRESIDENT OF THE UNITED STATES, by virtue of the power in me vested as **Commander-in-Chief of the Army and Navy** of the United States in time of actual armed Rebellion against the authority and government of the United States, and as a fit and necessary war measure for suppressing said Rebellion, do, on this first day of January, in the year of our Lord one thousand eight hundred and sixty-three, and in accordance with my purpose so to do, publicly proclaim for the full period of one hundred days from the day of the first above-mentioned order, and designate, as the States and parts of States wherein the people thereof respectively are this day in rebellion against the United States, the following, to wit: ARKANSAS, TEXAS, LOUISIANA (except the Parishes of St. Bernard, Plaquemines, Jefferson, St. John, St. Charles, St. James, Ascension, Assumption, Terre Bonne, La Fourche, St. Mary, St. Martin, and Orleans, including the City of Orleans), MISSISSIPPI, ALABAMA, FLORIDA, GEORGIA, SOUTH CAROLINA, NORTH CAROLINA, AND VIRGINIA (except the forty-eight counties designated as West Virginia, and also the counties of Berkeley, Accomac, Northampton, Elizabeth City, York, Princess Ann, and Norfolk, including the cities of Norfolk and Portsmouth), and which excepted parts are for the present left precisely as if this Proclamation were not issued.

And by virtue of the power and for the purpose aforesaid, I do order and declare that **ALL PERSONS HELD AS SLAVES** within said designated States and parts of States ARE, AND HENCEFORWARD **SHALL BE FREE!** and that the Executive Government of the United States, including the Military and Naval Authorities thereof, will RECOGNIZE AND MAINTAIN THE FREEDOM of said persons.

And I hereby enjoin upon the people so declared to be free, to abstain from all violence, UNLESS IN NECESSARY SELF-DEFENCE, and I recommend to them that in all cases, when allowed, they LABOR FAITHFULLY FOR REASONABLE WAGES.

And I further declare and make known that such persons of suitable condition will be received into the armed service of the United States, to garrison forts, positions, stations, and other places, and to man vessels of all sorts in said service.

And upon this act, SINCERELY BELIEVED TO BE AN ACT OF JUSTICE, warranted by the Constitution, upon military necessity, I invoke the considerate judgment of mankind, and the gracious favor of ALMIGHTY GOD.

In testimony whereof I have hereunto set my name, and caused the seal of the United States to be affixed.

[L. S.] Done at the CITY OF WASHINGTON, this first day of January, in the year of our Lord one thousand eight hundred and sixty-three, and of the Independence of the United States the eighty-seventh.

By the President.

A. Lincoln

William H. Seward

Secretary of State.

This reproduction of the Emancipation Proclamation can be found at the National Underground Railroad Freedom Center in Cincinnati.

largely accepted—except for the right of women of all colors to vote, which would later be addressed by the Nineteenth Amendment—and blacks were free to exercise their rights without the overhanging threat of fear and violence.

A sign designates where blacks are to wait for the bus in Durham, North Carolina, in 1940.

However, in the South during the 1950s, these liberties still were not extended. Civil War ideologies and racial discrimination lingered. Although blacks had been given freedom and rights decades earlier, for most people, **segregation** was a way of life, with **Jim Crow laws** in full effect. States and cities based these discriminatory laws on the idea of "separate but equal." Equal, however, was not part of the daily experience for African Americans in the Southern states. In most public places, blacks and whites were kept strictly apart. On buses, blacks were required by law to sit in the back and to give up their seats to whites if the bus was full. Most public places, such as movie theaters, restaurants, and waiting rooms in bus stations, had separate entrances and rules for serving blacks and whites. Black children attended inferior schools that did not present the same education or opportunities afforded to white children. In the courts, acts of violence against blacks by whites went largely unpunished, with rulings by all-white juries overseen by white judges. This system of **oppression** was maintained through intimidation and by blocking blacks' ability to vote and hold positions of power.

While people had been actively working toward overcoming segregation and creating equality for all races for decades, it was not until the mid-1950s that the civil rights movement began to fully take flight. At the head of this movement was Martin Luther King Jr., one of the most powerful leaders and influential **orators** of the era. His message of peaceful protest and nonviolence to bring about social change served as a cornerstone of the civil rights movement.

"Nonviolence is a powerful and just weapon. Indeed, it is a weapon unique in history, which cuts without wounding and ennobles the man who wields it," he said in his Nobel lecture in 1964.

Through his words, Martin Luther King Jr. ennobled us all.

CHAPTER ONE

The Man Behind the Marches

On January 15, 1929, Reverend Martin Luther King Sr. and his wife, Alberta Williams King, welcomed the arrival of their first son, Michael (which would later be changed to Martin) Luther King. He was born at 501 Auburn Avenue, in the two-story home shared by the Kings and Alberta's parents in Atlanta, Georgia. The neighborhood, known as "Sweet Auburn," was filled with middle-class African-American families. Reverend King and Alberta had three children: Christine, the eldest; Martin Luther Jr., shortened to M. L.; and Alfred Daniel, shortened to A. D. Growing up, Martin was especially close with his grandmother, whom he called Mama.

A Religious Upbringing

Religion formed the heart of the King family. Martin Sr. had taken over for Alberta's father as the minister at Ebenezer Baptist Church, one of Atlanta's largest African-American

The King family lived on Auburn Avenue until 1941. The house has been preserved as part of the Martin Luther King Jr. National Historic Site.

churches. Alberta served as the church's musical director. The three King children spent several days a week at Ebenezer. As a young boy, Martin was especially fond of singing, joining the church choir and belting out his favorite hymn, "I Want to Be More and More Like Jesus."

King's religious upbringing taught him to love his enemies and to meet hatred with love. Biblical passages such as Matthew 5:38–39 exemplify these lessons: "You have heard that it was said, 'Eye for eye, and tooth for tooth.' But I tell you, do not resist an evil person. If anyone slaps you on the right cheek, turn to them the other cheek also." These were lessons King would carry with him as he grew up. King later recalled how Sunday School at Ebenezer "helped me to build the capacity for getting along with people." Compassion and turning the other cheek to racial discrimination were lessons enforced by Martin Sr. and Alberta for all of their children.

Martin Luther King Sr. preached at Ebenezer Baptist Church until 1975.

An Early Encounter with Segregation

In Atlanta in the 1930s, segregation was a way of life. For his first few years, King was blissfully unaware of the division between the city's white and black communities. That all changed when the young boy experienced his first dose of segregation. For years, King had played with the son of a white shopkeeper who owned a store near the King home. When the boys turned six, they headed off to school—Martin to a blacks-only school, his friend to a school for white children. Shortly after, the boy's father forbade his son from playing with King. After King's parents explained that the boy's father did not want his son playing with Martin because he was black, the young boy grew angry. Alberta explained the system of segregation to her son, positioning it as a "social condition" rather than a "natural order." In the same lesson, she instilled in King a sense of "somebodiness." King described this as "the first time I was made aware of the existence of a race problem." Even at such a young age, King recognized the need to change the oppressive treatment of African Americans in the South. His older sister, Christine, remembered a fired-up Martin declaring to Alberta, "Mother dear, one day I'm going to turn this world upside down."

Powerful Words

King attended Booker T. Washington, the only African-American high school in Atlanta. He was a bright student and skipped two grades during his high school years. At fourteen, King traveled to Dublin, Georgia, with a schoolteacher to participate in a public speaking contest. His speech, entitled "The Negro and the Constitution," highlighted what would become King's ultimate goal: "[W]e may conquer Southern armies by the sword, but it is another thing to conquer Southern hate." King recognized the importance of overcoming hatred; he saw that change was needed at a deeper level than what could be achieved with force.

King's speech won first prize. What should have been a victorious trip home quickly dissolved with the sting of segregation. In ***The Autobiography** of Martin Luther King, Jr.*, King recounts the ride home to Atlanta. Incidents such as these would stay with King throughout his life:

> That night, Mrs. Bradley and I were on a bus returning to Atlanta. Along the way, some white passengers boarded the bus, and the white driver ordered us to get up and give the whites our seats. We didn't move quickly enough to suit him, so he began cursing us. I intended to stay right in that seat, but Mrs. Bradley urged me up, saying we had to obey the law. We stood up in the aisle for ninety miles to Atlanta. That night will never leave my memory. It was the angriest I have ever been in my life.

Morehouse College

In September 1944, King enrolled at Morehouse College, an all-male, all-black college in Atlanta, to study sociology. Attending Morehouse was somewhat of a family tradition; both King's father and grandfather has previously attended the school. At Morehouse, King studied the writings of great supporters of peaceful protest, including the 1849 essay "Civil Disobedience" by **abolitionist** Henry David Thoreau.

Dr. Benjamin Mays provided support and advice for Martin Luther King Jr.

While at Morehouse, King also found a mentor in Dr. Benjamin Mays, the college president and a Baptist minister like King's father. Mays was a strong supporter of civil rights and urged the members of his congregation to actively protest for social change. Throughout King's involvement in the civil rights campaign, Mays served as his advisor and as a pillar of support.

During the summer of his sophomore year at Morehouse, King composed a letter to the editor of the *Atlanta Constitution*, which appeared in the paper on August 6, 1946. King wrote:

> We want and are entitled to the basic rights and opportunities of American citizens: The right to earn a living at work for which we are fitted by training and ability; equal

Following Gandhi

Mohandas Karamchand Gandhi was born in India in 1869. After earning a law degree in London, England, Gandhi traveled to South Africa for work. There, he encountered social injustice under **apartheid**. Gandhi returned to India in 1915. To protest a British tax on salt, he led the Salt March to collect his own from the Arabian Sea. This was illegal under British law. In the 1930 march, which covered 240 miles (386.2 kilometers), Gandhi led tens of thousands of people to the water, where he and many of the others were arrested. He earned the nickname Mahatma, which means "great soul." Gandhi was assassinated on January 30, 1948, in New Delhi, India.

Mohandas Gandhi scoops a handful of salt after his long march to the Arabian Sea. He was protesting a tax on salt.

King traveled to India on a **pilgrimage** of sorts in 1959, further deepening his respect and belief in Gandhi's message of nonviolence. During a radio interview in India, King reflected on his visit: "Since being in India, I am more convinced than ever before that the method of nonviolent resistance is the most potent weapon available to oppressed people in their struggle for justice and human dignity."

> opportunities in education, health, recreation, and similar public services; the right to vote; equality before the law; some of the same courtesy and good manners that we ourselves bring to all human relations.

It is believed that King wrote this letter in response to racially motivated murders that were covered by the paper the month before. In the wake of these tragedies, King does not respond with anger or hatred. Rather, he clearly articulates the fundamental rights desired by African Americans. This letter offers a glimpse of the young man who would become the face of the fight for racial and social equality.

To the North

During his last year at Morehouse, in 1948, King was **ordained** as a Baptist minister. After graduating later that year, King headed north to pursue a bachelor of divinity degree at Crozer Theological Seminary in Chester, Pennsylvania. During breaks, he began working alongside his father as associate minister at Ebenezer. Throughout his time at Morehouse and Crozer, King studied many of the greatest thinkers of the past few centuries, trying to pair his religious upbringing with an effective philosophy for social change.

One Sunday, King traveled to nearby Philadelphia to hear a lecture on the great Indian leader Mahatma Gandhi and his teachings of nonviolence. Inspired, King left the lecture and purchased a half-dozen books on Gandhi's teachings. Gandhi's championing of nonviolence, and specifically his belief in satyagraha, or "truth force," resonated with the young student. Satyagraha is a philosophy that believes in the power of truth and love to bring about peaceful social change. King recalled how it was "in this Gandhian emphasis on love and nonviolence that I discovered the method for social reform that I had been seeking for so many months."

After completing his studies at Crozer, and serving as class valedictorian, King headed to Boston. There, he began working toward a PhD in theology, which was awarded to him by Boston University in 1955. Early in his time in Boston, King met a young music student named Coretta Scott. She had grown up on a farm in Marion, Alabama, then traveled to Ohio to attend Antioch College. From there, she moved to Boston to study at the New England Conservatory of Music. The two students clicked, and in 1953, they were married by Martin Luther King Sr. in Marion.

Back to the South

King knew his future lay in the South. In 1954, he accepted a position as the pastor of Dexter Avenue Baptist Church in the heavily segregated city of Montgomery, Alabama. The Kings settled into life in Montgomery, with the new preacher spending much of his time preparing Sunday sermons and working on his doctoral dissertation. Dexter Avenue's congregation was largely made up of influential blacks, and from the pulpit, King encouraged his congregation to register to vote and to join civil rights groups such as the National Association for the Advancement of Colored People (NAACP). King soon became acquainted with Ralph Abernathy, another Baptist minister.

Martin Luther King became the pastor of Dexter Avenue Baptist Church in 1954.

While King was completing his studies in Boston, the civil rights movement was energized

"All the News That's Fit to Print"

The New York Times.

LATE CITY EDITION

VOL. CIII... No. 35,178. NEW YORK, TUESDAY, MAY 18, 1954. FIVE CENTS

HIGH COURT BANS SCHOOL SEGREGATION; 9-TO-0 DECISION GRANTS TIME TO COMPLY

McCarthy Hearing Off a Week as Eisenhower Bars Report

SENATOR IS IRATE

President Orders Aides Not to Disclose Details of Top-Level Meeting

Communist Arms Unloaded in Guatemala By Vessel From Polish Port, U. S. Learns

State Department Views News Gravely Because of Red Infiltration

Embassy Says Nation of Central America May Buy Munitions Anywhere

REACTION OF SOUTH

'Breathing Spell' for Adjustment Tempers Region's Feelings

1896 RULING UPSET

'Separate but Equal' Doctrine Held Out of Place in Education

SOVIET BIDS VIENNA CEASE 'INTRIGUES'

Envoy Warns Austrian Chief on Inciting East Zone—Raab Denies Charges

City Colleges' Board Can't Pick Chairman

2 TAX PROJECTS DIE IN ESTIMATE BOARD

Beer Levy and More Parking Collections Killed—Payroll Impost Still Weighed

LEADERS IN SEGREGATION FIGHT: Lawyers who led battle before U. S. Supreme Court for abolition of segregation in public schools congratulate one another as they leave court after announcement of decision. Left to right: George E. C. Hayes, Thurgood Marshall and James M. Nabrit.

MORETTIS' LAWYER MUST BARE TALKS

Jersey Court Orders Counsel to Racketeers in Bergen to Divulge Data to Grand Jury

RULING TO FIGURE IN '54 CAMPAIGN

Decision Tied to Eisenhower—Russell Leads Southerners in Criticism of Court

INDO-CHINA PARLEY WEIGHS TWO PLANS

French and Rebel Peace Bids Will Be Studied Jointly as a Basis for Settlement

Costello Is Sentenced to 5 Years, Fined $30,000 in U. S. Tax Case

Churchill Asks Negotiated Peace With Guarantees for Indo-China

'Voice' Speaks in 34 Languages To Flash Court Ruling to World

The historic ruling on the *Brown v. Board of Education of Topeka* case made headlines across the United States.

by the ruling in the *Brown v. Board of Education of Topeka* case. This landmark case was the consolidation of five cases from Kansas, South Carolina, Delaware, Virginia, and the District of Columbia that fought for desegregation in public schools due to the inferior conditions in all-black schools. On May 17, 1954, the US Supreme Court handed down its unanimous decision, declaring "in the field of public education, the doctrine of 'separate but equal' has no place. Separate educational facilities are inherently unequal."

This decision set a promising **precedent** for future segregation cases. It ruled that the US Constitution officially supported equality between blacks and whites and declared segregation in schools **unconstitutional**. In a later speech, King referred to the landmark decision as "a legal and sociological deathblow to an evil that has occupied the throne of American life for several decades." Even with the Supreme Court's ruling, it would take decades for schools and other public facilities across the South to desegregate.

Following the *Brown* ruling, Montgomery civil rights leaders were eager to use this forward momentum to address segregation in Alabama's capital. This opportunity came the following year, on December 1, 1955. That evening, forty-two-year-old Rosa Parks boarded a bus to head home after a long day of work as a seamstress at a local department store. As the bus rolled through Montgomery, the seats began to fill. Soon, all of the white seats at the front of the bus were taken. By law, blacks were required to give up their seats once the front whites-only section was filled. When a white man boarded, the driver ordered the four blacks sitting in the first row of the colored section to give up their seats. Parks refused. The police were called, and she was arrested and fined. Little did anyone know how this small act of defiance would soon launch King into a new role as the voice of the civil rights movement.

CHAPTER TWO

The Call to Action

Martin Luther King Jr. lent the power of his words in support of Rosa Parks. A women's activist group handed out pamphlets urging blacks to **boycott** Montgomery's buses on Monday, December 5, the day of Parks's trial, to protest the woman's arrest. Support for the planned boycott spread quickly. In Sunday services, preachers urged their congregations to stay off the buses the following day, and black taxi companies showed their support by offering to match their fares to what the bus would normally cost.

The boycott was more successful than many expected. Come Monday morning, most of the buses, normally filled with blacks, rumbled through the streets of Montgomery empty. Nearly all the blacks in Montgomery carpooled, took taxis, or even walked to work instead of taking the bus. Outside the courthouse, hundreds of blacks showed up to support Parks, who was convicted. Her lawyer filed an appeal, which got tied up in the courts.

Rosa Parks sat for a police photograph following her arrest for not yielding her seat on a Montgomery bus.

After the success of the one-day boycott, leaders in the black community met to discuss a plan to challenge the law on bus segregation. A single day of lost business for the bus line would not be enough to send a strong message. To organize a successful, long-term boycott, organization and leadership were needed. The Montgomery Improvement Association (MIA) was quickly formed, with twenty-six-year-old King elected as its president. The association immediately set to work drafting a formal arrangement for the boycott.

The MIA drew up its plan for the boycott in the form of a resolution, which it sent to city officials on December 6. The document asked that all citizens stop riding buses owned by Montgomery City Lines Inc., that people with cars help get others to work without charge, and that employers provide transportation for their workers. It also said that black citizens were ready to discuss and work out their grievances.

The message was clear: until the treatment of blacks aboard city buses changed, Montgomery's African-American community would not be riding those buses.

381 Days of Boycott

The boycott was met with hostility. King and other members of the MIA quickly came to realize that city officials were not interested in change. As the days passed, the MIA worked to establish a carpool of three hundred cars owned by blacks and a system to shuttle people to and from work. As the days turned into weeks, the city tried to force an end to the carpool system, arresting King and a number of other blacks for organizing the boycott, which was illegal under a city law. King was found guilty; however, his lawyer quickly appealed the conviction.

During the boycott, a bus carrying only a couple of white women travels through Montgomery in March 1956.

In the fall, city officials declared the carpool a public nuisance, but that tactic was undercut by some fortunate news. While Parks's case was bogged down in the state court of appeals, a panel of judges in a US district court, hearing another case on public bus segregation, ruled that bus segregation was unconstitutional. The case, *Browder v. Gayle*, reached the US Supreme Court. On November 13, 1956, the Supreme Court justices agreed with the district court panel: the segregated bus laws in Alabama were unconstitutional, and therefore illegal. On December 21, King was one of the first black people to ride aboard a newly integrated Montgomery bus. After 381 days, the bus boycott was over.

Martin Luther King Jr. appeals for calm after an angry mob formed outside his home, which was damaged by a bomb.

King and his family were constantly the target of violence and death threats. Menacing phone calls and letters became commonplace in the King household. Despite these violent threats, King refused personal protection and greeted those who wished him harm with compassion. During the Montgomery bus boycott, King's home was bombed, with Coretta and their baby daughter Yolanda inside. They escaped uninjured. An angry mob of blacks formed in front of the parsonage. Standing in front of the wreckage, King pled for nonviolence, saying:

> If you have weapons, take them home; if you do not have them, please do not seek

them. We cannot solve this problem through retaliatory violence. We must meet violence with nonviolence … Love your enemies; bless them that curse you; pray for them that despitefully use you … Remember, if I am stopped, this movement will not stop, because God is with the movement.

Putting Words to Action

Through physical acts of defiance, King paired his Gandhian principles of peaceful protest with the power of **direct action**, staged in boycotts, marches, and sit-ins throughout the 1950s and 1960s. In a 1958 speech on nonviolence, King said, "A boycott is never an end within itself. It is merely a means to awaken a sense of shame within the oppressor but the end is reconciliation, the end is redemption." His goal was to get those who enacted laws to segregate and oppress blacks to renounce that bigotry. Additionally, King saw direct action as a means to force the federal government to intervene in matters that directly violated black citizens' constitutional rights.

On the heels of the success in Montgomery, boycotts were organized in three more cities: Birmingham and Mobile in Alabama, and Tallahassee in Florida. King and other pastors believed that a central organization focusing on civil rights was needed, and thus the Southern Christian Leadership Conference (SCLC) was founded in January 1957. Originally called the Southern Negro Leaders Conference on Transportation and Nonviolent Integration, its first membership was made up of sixty black leaders from ten Southern states.

The mission of the group, outlined in a document titled "A Statement to the South and Nation," urges all blacks "no matter how great the obstacles and suffering … to reject segregation." The need for nonviolence is reinforced by the SCLC instructing blacks to abide by the motto "Not one hair of one head of one white person shall be harmed." It closes with a reference to the national anthem, saying that with the achievement of equality, all Americans "shall be emotionally relieved and freed to turn our energies to making America truly 'The land of the free and the home of the brave.'"

"Give Us the Ballot"

After Montgomery, and with the newly established SCLC ready for action, King was flooded with invitations to speak across the country. Voting rights for blacks soon became a top issue. One of King's earliest national addresses focused on empowering change through the power of voting. In 1957, at the Prayer Pilgrimage for Freedom, from the steps of the Lincoln Memorial in Washington, DC, King gave his "Give Us the Ballot" speech.

> Give us the ballot, and we will no longer have to worry the federal government about our basic rights.
>
> Give us the ballot, and we will no longer plead to the federal government for passage of an anti-lynching law; we will by the power of our vote write the law on the statute books of the South and bring an end to the dastardly acts of the hooded perpetrators of violence.
>
> Give us the ballot, and we will transform the salient misdeeds of bloodthirsty mobs into the calculated good deeds of orderly citizens.
>
> Give us the ballot, and we will fill our legislative halls with men of goodwill and send to the sacred halls of Congress men who will not sign a "Southern Manifesto" because of their devotion to the manifesto of justice.
>
> Give us the ballot, and we will place judges on the benches of the South who will do justly

> and love mercy, and we will place at the head of the Southern states governors who will, who have felt not only the tang of the human, but the glow of the Divine.
>
> Give us the ballot, and we will quietly and nonviolently, without rancor or bitterness, implement the Supreme Court's decision of May seventeenth, 1954.

King was saying that if it were possible for blacks to exercise their voting rights, America's black community would solve the issues of segregation through the democratic system already in place. This early speech highlights one of King's largest goals within the civil rights movement.

Riding for Freedom

The spirit of the civil rights movement became infectious. In the spring of 1961, students from the Congress for Racial Equality (CORE) set out to challenge segregation on interstate buses—and the terminals where they stopped—across the South.

The precedent set by two Supreme Court cases lay the foundation for the CORE campaign. In 1946, the Court had ruled in the *Morgan v. Virginia* case that segregation on interstate travel was unconstitutional. The issue was taken one step further in 1960, with the *Boynton v. Virginia* ruling that declared segregation was also illegal in establishments that served travelers, including terminals, restrooms, and restaurants. In 1961, however, despite these rulings, segregation on buses and in terminals was alive and well in the South.

The first "Freedom Ride," made up of both black and white students, pulled out of Washington, DC, in two buses on May 4. Their goal: to draw attention to the fact that laws prohibiting segregation were not enforced during interstate

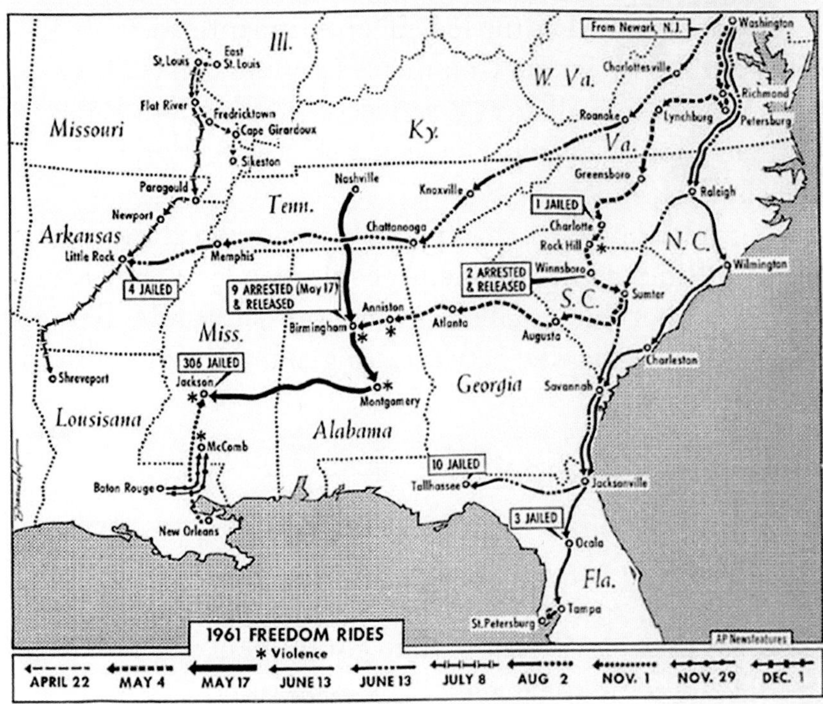

This map produced by the Associated Press shows the routes taken by the Freedom Rides and details where its participants were met with violence.

travel. They faced violence and arrest in Rock Hill, South Carolina; in Anniston, Alabama; in Birmingham; and finally in Montgomery, where a police escort didn't show up and the riders were attacked. Several were severely beaten.

King led a rally for the riders at the First Baptist Church in Montgomery. Among those in attendance were the pastor Ralph Abernathy and future congressman John Lewis. During the rally, a crowd of angry white people gathered outside the church. Fearing further violence, King called US attorney general Robert F. Kennedy. He and his brother President John F. Kennedy convinced the governor to send in the Alabama National Guard to protect the people trapped inside the church. At dawn the following morning, people were escorted home.

By the end of May, the federal government had instructed the Interstate Commerce Commission (ICC) to ban segregation in all areas it serviced. The Freedom Rides continued until November 1, when anti-segregation laws officially took effect.

King and the SCLC had publicly championed the Freedom Rides. However, many people wondered why King himself did not ride or take a much more active role. Tensions were beginning to grow between King and the more **militant** student activists.

Birmingham Campaign

While King remained active in the civil rights movement for the next two years, including leading another campaign in Georgia, his powerful presence was still much needed in Alabama. There, in 1963, the state government was holding firm against ending segregation.

That spring, the SCLC attacked Birmingham's segregation laws with a massive campaign. The city of Birmingham was considered to be the most racially segregated town in the South. The push for equality included a boycott of downtown businesses, marches, sit-ins at lunch counters, and mass meetings, during which King appealed for volunteers. Hundreds of protestors were jailed.

On April 10, city officials received an **injunction** from the state, making the protests illegal. In direct defiance, the protests continued. King chose to risk arrest as a "faith act" to show his commitment to the cause. On April 12, King was arrested and placed in solitary confinement. The day of his arrest, a letter appeared in the *Birmingham News* from eight white clergymen, criticizing King and his methods.

The letter called for the end of black protests, describing them as "unwise and untimely." The clergymen advocated the courts as the appropriate arena for the segregation issue,

Blocking Entrance

Segregation as public policy was supported in the South long after "separate but equal" was struck down by the Supreme Court.

In the most famous speech uttered in support of segregation, newly elected Alabama governor George C. Wallace declared in his inaugural address on January 14, 1963:

> In the name of the greatest people that have ever trod this earth, I draw a line in the dust and toss the gauntlet before the feet of tyranny, and I say, segregation now, segregation tomorrow, and segregation forever.

These words were well received by white Southerners. Don Carter, the historian who wrote a biography about Wallace titled *The Politics of Rage*, remembered that Wallace supporters filled the streets of Montgomery to hear the speech and showed their dedication to white supremacy by wearing white flowers.

Later that year, Wallace led a move to "stand in the schoolhouse door" to keep two black students from enrolling in the University of Alabama. The students enrolled only after the National Guard stepped in.

not the streets of Birmingham. It went on to undermine the act of protest, painting the demonstrations as "actions as to incite hatred and violence, however technically peaceful those actions may be …"

The letter closes:

> We further strongly urge our own Negro community to withdraw support from these demonstrations, and to unite locally in working peacefully for a better Birmingham. When rights are consistently denied, a cause should be pressed in the courts and in negotiations among local leaders, and not in the streets. We appeal to both our white and Negro citizenry to observe the principles of law and order and common sense.

A copy of the paper was smuggled in to King. During his eight-day imprisonment, King penned his response, the "Letter from Birmingham Jail," in the margins of the paper. He explains the purpose behind the campaign's direct action:

> You may well ask: "Why direct action? Why sit-ins, marches, etc? Isn't negotiation a better path?" You are exactly right in your call for negotiation. Indeed, this is the very purpose of direct action. Nonviolent direct action seeks to create such a crisis and establish such creative tension that a community which has constantly refused to negotiate is forced to confront the issue. It seeks so to dramatize the issue that it can no longer be ignored. I just referred to the creation of tension as part of the work of the nonviolent resister. This may sound rather shocking. But I must confess that I am not afraid of the word tension. I have earnestly worked and preached against violent tension, but there is a type of constructive, nonviolent tension that is necessary for growth.

Police used water canons and dogs to attack young people protesting segregation in Birmingham in May 1963.

The Birmingham campaign was not over. On May 2, more than one thousand children took to the streets in the Children's Crusade. There, they met snarling dogs, high-pressure hoses, and the blows of police clubs. With pressure mounting to end the conflict, a compromise was reached which included the commitment of a plan to desegregate lunch counters, increase employment opportunities of blacks, and release protestors from prison.

While the campaign was successful to a degree, violence still ran deep in the city. After the campaign, the room where King and other SCLC members had been staying was bombed. The home of King's brother, A. D., was also the target of a bombing.

To Washington

Many civil rights leaders were growing frustrated with the federal government's lack of support for a new civil rights

Martin Luther King Jr. responds to a warm welcome at the March on Washington on August 28, 1963.

bill. The March on Washington for Jobs and Freedom took place on August 28, 1963, drawing about 250,000 people. The highlight of the day was King's famous "I Have a Dream" speech. After the march, King and other leaders met with President Kennedy at the White House. Many of these issues highlighted at the march were addressed the following year in the monumental Civil Rights Act of 1964.

Despite the progress the movement had made, racial hatred still ran deep in the South. Just one month after the March on Washington, members of the KKK bombed the Sixteenth Street Baptist Church in Birmingham, killing four young black girls. King gave the eulogy at a funeral service for three of the victims.

Bloody Sunday

In January 1965, the SCLC joined forces with other activist groups to set up a voting rights campaign in Selma, Alabama. In Selma, only 2 percent of black people were documented on voting rolls as blacks faced immense discrimination when trying to register to vote. In January and February, peaceful marches were held. On February 26, the violence escalated during an evening march in nearby Marion. During the struggle, twenty-six-year-old Jimmie Lee Johnson was shot while trying to protect his mother from the blows of a nightstick. He died eight days later.

A march was organized for March 7 to walk from Selma to the steps of the state capitol in Montgomery, 50 miles (80.5 km) away. King was not present at the march, as he was in Atlanta on other SCLC business. The march made its way through the streets of Selma with no resistance, until protesters reached the Edmund Pettus Bridge. There, local authorities were waiting for them. The marchers were ordered to disband and end the protest. When the marchers peacefully refused, the state and local authorities attacked the unarmed group with tear gas and clubs. Police on horseback continued to beat protesters as they fled in terror. The violent attack, which became known as Bloody Sunday, shocked the nation.

John Lewis, who suffered a skull fracture in the attack, provided a firsthand account of the violence under questioning by an attorney identified only as Hall during a hearing on March 17:

> Lewis: I was hit on my head right here.
> Hall: What were you hit with?
> Lewis: I was hit with a billy club, and I saw the State Trooper that hit me.
> Hall: How many times were you hit?
> Lewis: I was hit twice, once when I was lying

John Lewis (*kneeling in the foreground*) suffers a skull fracture while being beaten by an Alabama state trooper in Selma.

down and was attempting to get up.
Hall: Do we understand you to say you were hit
... and then attempted to get up
and were hit—and was hit again?
Lewis: Right.

A Call for Help

King believed in rallying support from as many people as possible—regardless of the color of their skin. The evening of March 7, he began mailing out letters to religious leaders across the United States, urging them to come to Selma to march. In the message, King calls upon "clergy of all faiths representative of every part of the country, to join me for a ministers' march to Montgomery on Tuesday morning, March 9th."

President Lyndon B. Johnson urged King to postpone the march so the federal government could offer protection to the marchers. However, the march went ahead as planned. King led a crowd of two thousand to the bridge, where police forces lay waiting. There, in a surprising act, King led a prayer on bended knee, then turned and walked back to Selma.

Impelled by the violence in Selma, President Johnson gave a speech supporting the marchers on March 15. Early in his address, Johnson said, "There is no Negro problem. There is no Southern problem. There is no Northern problem. There is only an American problem."

Following Johnson's speech, and the introduction of a new voting rights act in Congress, a final march left Selma on March 21, under the federal government's protection. Four days later, King and his fellow protesters at last reached the steps of the state capitol.

CHAPTER THREE

The World Reacts

As the face of the civil rights movement, King was constantly appearing in the media: in newspaper stories, on television shows, and in radio interviews. This very public role was not always an easy one to fill. As often as King was greeted with words of praise and hailed as a national hero, so too did he receive criticism—from both blacks and whites, from all walks of life.

Toward the end of the 1960s, King began to broaden his focus beyond civil rights to include human rights. He strongly opposed US participation in the Vietnam War. On April 4, 1967, King delivered his speech "Beyond Vietnam" to a crowd of three thousand at Riverside Church in New York City. When the US military first became active in Southeast Asia in 1965, many civil rights organizations had issued statements distinguishing their cause from the distant conflict. For King, however, the two were linked; the war in Vietnam was "taking the black young men who had been crippled by our society and

The Chicago newspaper headline on August 19, 1966, stated, "City Seeks to Cut Marches," but Martin Luther King Jr. and his aide, Reverend Jesse Jackson, did not back down.

sending them eight thousand miles away to guarantee liberties in Southeast Asia which they had not found in southwest Georgia and East Harlem." For King, it was unacceptable that the United States could spend millions to send troops abroad, yet they could not protect people from violence and discrimination in the South. These sentiments did not earn King much support.

The struggle for equal rights was not restricted to just the United States. In 1957, Martin Luther King Jr. and his wife, Coretta Scott King, traveled to Ghana to celebrate the African nation's independence from British colonialism. Upon meeting US vice president Richard Nixon, King used the opportunity to draw parallels between Ghana gaining its independence and the ongoing civil rights struggle in the South, saying, "I want you to come visit us down in Alabama

Martin Luther King Jr. was awarded the Nobel Peace Prize in 1964.

where we are seeking the same kind of freedom the Gold Coast is celebrating." The trip also gave King new vigor in the American struggle; if Ghanaian independence was attainable, surely, too, was equality for black Americans.

The international community hailed King as a hero. On December 10, 1964, King traveled to Oslo, Norway, to accept one of the most highly regarded awards in the world: the Nobel Peace Prize. At thirty-five, King was the youngest person to ever receive the prestigious award. King humbly accepted the award on behalf of the civil rights movement.

King Under Investigation

Throughout the 1950s and 1960s, King came under the watch of the Federal Bureau of Investigation (FBI). J. Edgar Hoover, the FBI's director, harbored a strong dislike for King, believing he associated with communists. There was also a fear of the power of King's leadership, with some officials referring to him as a "black messiah." Hoover was determined to take down the civil rights leader. For years, King's offices and hotel rooms were wiretapped. No evidence of communist activity was ever

Martin Luther King Jr. and other civil rights leaders gathered in the White House alongside President John F. Kennedy following the March on Washington.

recorded. However, much was captured of King's personal life, including extramarital affairs. These personal matters were leveraged to try to remove King from the civil rights campaign. In 1964, a compromising tape recording and an anonymous letter were sent to King by the FBI; the SCLC staff believed the letter urged King to commit suicide. King, however, did not allow this personal attack to sway him from his cause.

King and Kennedy

At the federal level, King's message of peaceful protest was admired by some yet despised by others. Over several years, King developed a relationship with President John F. Kennedy, who held the presidency from January 1961 until his assassination in November 1963.

Kennedy walked a fine line in his support of King's cause before he became president; while he knew that civil rights would inevitably need to be addressed, he also relied on many cities in the South for support at the polls. While King was imprisoned during a 1960 Atlanta sit-in, the then senator placed a call to Coretta. He was among a group, which also included Robert Kennedy, who helped secure King's release. Kennedy would introduce the Civil Rights Act to Congress in 1963 after the violent demonstrations in Birmingham. Following the March on Washington, King was among a group of civil rights leaders invited to the White House.

The Rise of Black Power

By the mid-1960s, the long journey to equality had grown tiresome for some blacks. A divide was growing between leading organizations of the civil rights movement. Some felt that peaceful demonstrations were not effective or took too long to bring about changes to **legislation**.

Among the leaders of this way of thinking was Malcolm X, a militant black leader during the civil rights era. Born Malcolm Little in Omaha, Nebraska, his tumultuous childhood was riddled with racial discrimination. The Little house was burned to the ground, and Malcolm X's father, a Baptist minister, was believed to have been murdered by white supremacists. While serving time in prison as an adult, Malcolm X became a Muslim and joined the Nation of Islam (NOI), an African-American group which paired the Islamic faith with black **nationalism**. He also changed his last name to X as a rejection of the name given to his slave ancestors by their owners.

Black nationalism was a philosophy that stated that black people should control the politics and the economy in black communities. It dismissed the idea of desegregation and actually advocated the segregation of the races.

Malcolm became a minister, rising in the ranks until he became the public face of the NOI. His popularity, combined with his feeling that the leader of the NOI, Elijah Muhammad, was not doing enough for civil rights, caused a rift between the two men. Malcolm X left the NOI and founded the Organization of Afro-American Unity.

Elijah Muhammad, the leader of the Nation of Islam, disagreed with Martin Luther King Jr. on many issues.

Within this growing divide, King's commitment to peaceful protest was often criticized. Malcolm X held many of the same end goals as King. He, too, spoke and demonstrated for equal rights for blacks—although Malcolm X did not see the path to equality as one achieved through peaceful sit-ins and friendship with white Americans. He instead believed that peaceful protest was futile, saying "Tactics based solely on morality can only succeed when you are dealing with people who are moral or a system that is moral. A man or system which oppresses a man because of his color is not moral."

While these two leaders did not always agree on the most effective way to achieve civil rights, each man held the other in high regard. During King's imprisonment in Selma in early February 1965, Malcolm X traveled to the city to have a private meeting with Coretta. As recalled by Coretta in her autobiography *My Life with Martin Luther King, Jr.*, Malcolm X told her, "I really did come thinking that I could make it easier. If the white people realize what the alternative is, perhaps they will be more willing to hear Dr. King." In this instance, the threat of violent action against segregation would be used to promote King's message of peaceful protest as a better alternative—for both blacks and whites.

On February 21, 1965, Malcolm X was assassinated by followers of the NOI during a speaking engagement at the Audubon Ballroom in Manhattan.

Although King and Malcolm X corresponded, they met only once, during a conference at the US Senate.

Peaceful Protest vs. Violent Resistance

Many of Malcolm X's most famous speeches stand in stark contrast to King's philosophy of nonviolence. In response to the anthem of the movement, "We Shall Overcome," which King often quoted in his speeches, Malcolm X famously said, "We want freedom now, but we're not going to get it saying 'We Shall Overcome.' We've got to fight to overcome."

In contrast to King's 1957 "Give Us the Ballot" address, Malcolm X took a much more divided viewpoint in his "Ballot or the Bullet" speech delivered in 1964:

> Why does it look like it might be the year of the ballot or the bullet? Because Negroes have listened to the trickery, and the lies, and the

false promises of the white man now for too long. And they're fed up. They've become disenchanted. They've become disillusioned. They've become dissatisfied, and all of this has built up frustrations in the black community that makes the black community throughout America today more explosive than all of the atomic bombs the Russians can ever invent. Whenever you got a racial powder keg sitting in your lap, you're in more trouble than if you had an atomic powder keg sitting in your lap. When a racial powder keg goes off, it doesn't care who it knocks out the way. Understand this, it's dangerous.

In 1967, at a convention marking the SCLC's eleventh year, King addressed the growing divide between civil rights groups:

I say to you today that I still stand by nonviolence. And I'm still convinced that it is the most potent weapon available to the Negro in his struggle for justice in this country.

And the other thing is, I'm concerned about a better world. I'm concerned about justice; I'm concerned about brotherhood; I'm concerned about truth. And when one is concerned about that, he can never advocate violence. For through violence you may murder a murderer, but you can't murder murder. Through violence you may murder a liar, but you can't establish truth. Through violence you may murder a hater, but you can't murder hate through violence. Darkness cannot put out darkness; only light can do that.

CHAPTER FOUR

The March Goes On

In 1968, King and the SCLC began working with sanitation workers on strike in Memphis, Tennessee, to gain better working conditions. During a march he led on March 28, a group of protesters began breaking shop windows and police moved in violently. A sixteen-year-old, Larry Payne, was shot to death by police. King considered not returning to see the movement through. However, he realized his presence was needed more than ever. On April 3, King arrived back in Memphis. He spoke to a group of sanitation workers, delivering his famous "I've Been to the Mountaintop" speech.

The next evening, while preparing to attend a dinner at a local minister's home, King stepped onto the balcony outside of his room at the Lorraine Motel. An assassin fired a single shot, and the bullet struck King in the lower face. The civil rights leader was rushed to the hospital, but the wound was fatal. King, only thirty-nine years old, was pronounced dead. Ultimately, his iconic role within the civil rights movement

Police arrest a black man suspected of looting after violence broke out during a protest in support of sanitation workers on March 28, 1968, in Memphis, Tennessee.

Shocked civil rights leaders frantically point in the direction from which the shot that felled Martin Luther King Jr. was fired.

cost him his life, a price he had repeatedly said he was willing to pay for the cause in which he so deeply believed.

King's death shook the nation. In the days following, more than one hundred US cities erupted in violent riots, the worst of which were in Chicago, Baltimore, and Washington, DC. Headlines announced the tragedy to a shocked nation. The National Guard was deployed to several cities to stop the violence and looting. From Washington, DC, President Johnson addressing the nation, asking "every citizen to reject the blind violence that has struck Dr. King, who lived by nonviolence."

In another address, from Indianapolis, Indiana, Senator Robert F. Kennedy delivered a moving speech, attempting to unite all Americans in the wake of the tragedy, with the aim to stop any outbreaks of violence. In the speech, he recognized King's assassination as a **pivotal** point in the civil rights movement, and as an opportunity to "ask what kind of a nation we are and what direction we want to move in." Kennedy went on to empathize with the reaction of blacks—with their feelings of bitterness, hatred, and "a desire for revenge." He identified with these feelings:

> We can move in that direction as a country, in greater polarization—black people amongst blacks, and white amongst whites, filled with hatred toward one another. Or we can make an effort, as Martin Luther King did, to understand, and to comprehend, and replace that violence, that stain of bloodshed that has spread across our land, with an effort to understand, compassion, and love.
>
> For those of you who are black and are tempted to … be filled with hatred and mistrust of the injustice of such an act, against all white people, I would only say that I can also feel in my own heart the same kind of feeling. I had a member of my family killed, but he was killed by a white man.

Following Kennedy's speech, Indianapolis remained one of the few cities where no violence took place.

In the shadow of King's death, the cause he so deeply supported was not forgotten. On April 8, Coretta and other King family members led a silent march of about forty-two thousand people through the streets of Memphis in remembrance of King and in support of the city's sanitation workers.

Thousands of mourners follow behind Martin Luther King Jr.'s funeral procession through the streets of Atlanta.

Mourning Martin Luther King Jr.

King's body was returned to Atlanta. On April 9, 1968, his funeral was held at Ebenezer Baptist Church, which was filled to capacity, with thousands more lining the surrounding streets. At the service, a tape of King's final speech, delivered on April 3 in Memphis, was played. In some ways, King's speech seems to foreshadow his upcoming death:

> I've seen the promised land. I may not get there with you. But I want you to know tonight, that we, as a people, will get to the promised land. And so I'm happy, tonight. I'm not worried about anything. I'm not fearing any man. Mine eyes have seen the glory of the coming of the Lord.

After the service, King's body was carried on a wooden wagon pulled by two mules to Morehouse College. Along the 3.5-mile (5.6 km) route, more than one hundred thousand mourners paid their last respects to King. At Morehouse, a heavy-hearted Benjamin Mays delivered the eulogy, in which he urged people everywhere to carry on the work of King. At the end of the ceremony, the song "We Shall Overcome" served as the final farewell to the man who had changed the face of civil rights.

King was buried at South View Cemetery in Atlanta, with a memorial stone quoting his "I Have a Dream" speech: "Free at last, free at last; thank God Almighty, we are free at last." In 1977, his casket was relocated to the King Center, near Ebenezer Baptist Church, where it remains today.

Landmark Legislation

King always recognized that the end goal of the marches, freedom rides, boycotts, and sit-ins was to evoke new legislation

Coretta Scott King stands at the right hand of President Ronald Reagan as he signs the bill designating Martin Luther King Jr. Day as a national holiday.

Martin Luther King Jr. Day

Just four days after King's death, Congressman John Conyers introduced a proposal to institute a national holiday, celebrated on King's birthday, to remember the work of the great civil rights leader. Coretta Scott King quickly added her support to the idea, and on January 15, 1969, the King Center sponsored the first celebration to honor the great man's legacy. A bill in favor of the holiday was passed in Congress in fall 1983 and was signed into law shortly thereafter.

Each year, on the third Monday of January, the life and works of King are commemorated. It is a "day on," not a day off, on which many people participate in community service activities. The day is also recognized in more than one hundred places around the world. Through this holiday, King's legacy carries on in the work of those who continue to seek love and understanding and to break down social barriers.

Martin Luther King Jr. stands behind President Lyndon Johnson as he signs the historic Civil Rights Act into law on July 2, 1964.

at the federal level that would outlaw the glaring bigotry supported by local and state governments across the South. King and other civil rights leaders saw the one hundredth anniversary of Lincoln's Emancipation Proclamation—1963—as a fitting year for the federal government to take a firm stance against segregation. The Birmingham campaign and March on Washington were two key events in pushing the government to make these reforms, which came in the groundbreaking legislation of the Civil Rights Act of 1964, introduced by John F. Kennedy in June 1963.

After Kennedy's assassination, President Johnson saw the bill carried through Congress, despite much resistance from several Southern politicians. The act drew a hard line against segregation, with no room for "separate but equal" ideologies.

Title II specifically made segregation illegal in public facilities, such as restaurants, movie theaters, hotels, and gas stations, stating that:

> Sec. 201 (a) All persons shall be entitled to the full and equal enjoyment of the goods, services, facilities, privileges, advantages, and accommodations of any place of public accommodation, as defined in this section, without discrimination or segregation on the ground of race, color, religion, or national origin.

The second and third sections go on to make any segregation laws established by local or state governments illegal, as well as any attempts to threaten a person exercising their rights:

> Sec 202. All persons shall be entitled to be free, at any establishment or place, from discrimination or segregation of any kind on the ground of race, color, religion, or national origin, if such discrimination or segregation is or purports to be required by any law, statute, ordinance, regulation, rule, or order of a State or any agency of political subdivision thereof.
> Sec. 203. No person shall (a) withhold, deny, or attempt to withhold or deny, or deprive or attempt to deprive, any person of any right or privilege secured by section 201 or 202, or (b) intimidate, threaten, or coerce, or attempt to intimidate, threaten, or coerce any person with the purpose of interfering with any right or privilege secured by section 201 or 202, or (c) punish or attempt to punish any person exercising or attempting to exercise any right or privilege secured by section 201 or 202.

Dr. Martin Luther King Jr. is buried beside the peaceful waters of a reflecting pool at the King Center in Atlanta. Coretta Scott King was buried alongside her husband following her death in 2006.

Following closely after the Civil Rights Act was the Voting Rights Act of 1965, which protected the rights of all people to vote without discrimination.

King Center for Nonviolent Social Change

To honor her late husband's legacy, in 1968, Coretta founded the Martin Luther King, Jr. Center for Nonviolent Social Change. The center carries on King's message of peaceful protest through education and as a living memorial. Using King's writings and teachings, the center identifies three "Triple Evils" working against equality: poverty, racism, and militarism. King outlined his six principles of nonviolence, which frame his way to fight injustice, in his book *Stride Toward Freedom*:

Principle One: Nonviolence is a way of life for courageous people. It is active nonviolent resistance to evil. It is aggressive spiritually, mentally and emotionally.

Principle Two: Nonviolence seeks to win friendship and understanding. The end result of nonviolence is redemption and reconciliation. The purpose of nonviolence is the creation of the **Beloved Commmunity**.

Principle Three: Nonviolence seeks to defeat injustice not people. Nonviolence recognizes that evildoers are also victims and are not evil people. The nonviolent resister seeks to defeat evil not people.

Principle Four: Nonviolence holds that suffering can educate and transform.
Nonviolence accepts suffering without retaliation. Unearned suffering is redemptive and has tremendous educational and transforming possibilities.

Principle Five: Nonviolence chooses love instead of hate. Nonviolence resists violence of the spirit as well as the body. Nonviolent love is spontaneous, unmotivated, unselfish and creative.

Principle Six: Nonviolence believes that the universe is on the side of justice.
The nonviolent resister has deep faith that justice will eventually win.
Nonviolence believes that God is a God of justice.

These six principles summarize King's enduring message of peace: choose love over hate, justice over injustice, and reconciliation over conflict. King recognized that the path of nonviolence was not an easy one, but one that "accepts suffering without retaliation" and has "transforming responsibilities."

Another Step Forward

Perhaps the greatest legacy left by King and his championing of peaceful protest is the message to carry on. From staying off the bus in Montgomery to walking into violence in the streets of Birmingham and Selma, he recognized that the path to equality was a long journey. Through his powerful words, unwavering leadership, and commitment to nonviolence, King ensured that more than one hundred years after they were written, these words from the Emancipation Proclamation were finally enacted, that "all persons held as slaves … are, and henceforward shall be free." Free to vote, free from discrimination, and free to pursue the greatest of American rights: life, liberty, and the pursuit of happiness.

Chronology

Dates in green pertain to events discussed in this volume.

1863 The Emancipation Proclamation is issued by President Abraham Lincoln.

1865 The Thirteenth Amendment, abolishing slavery, is passed in the US House of Representatives. The amendment was passed by the Senate in 1864.

1868 The Fourteenth Amendment, guaranteeing equal rights under the law, is passed.

1870 The Fifteenth Amendment, prohibiting governments from denying male citizens the right to vote based on their race, is passed.

1883 Supreme Court strikes down the Civil Rights Act of 1875, which guaranteed equal rights to all African Americans in transportation, restaurant or inns, theaters, and on juries.

1896 *Plessy v. Ferguson*, establishing the precedent of "separate but equal," is handed down by the Supreme Court of the United States.

1900 In a fourteen-year period ending at the turn of the century, more than 2,500 African Americans are lynched, most in the Deep South.

1909 The National Association for the Advancement of Colored People (NAACP) is established.

1929 Martin Luther King Jr. is born in Atlanta, Georgia, on January 15.

1935 Thurgood Marshall and Charles Hamilton Houston successfully sue the University of Maryland, arguing for Donald Murray's admission to the institution's law school in *Murray v. Pearson*. The two argue that as the state does not provide a public law school for African Americans, it does not provide adequate "separate but equal" institutions.

1941 President Franklin D. Roosevelt bans discrimination against minorities in the granting of defense contracts.

1947 Jackie Robinson breaks the color barrier, becoming the first African American to play in Major League Baseball.

1948 Martin Luther King Jr. is ordained and begins work as the assistant pastor at Ebenezer Baptist Church in Atlanta.

1953 King marries Coretta Scott on June 18.

1954 Thurgood Marshall and the NAACP win the case of *Brown v. Board of Education of Topeka*, which overturns *Plessy v.*

Ferguson and the "separate but equal" doctrine of segregation in the United States.

1955 Rosa Parks refuses on December 1 to give up her seat to a white person on a bus in Montgomery, Alabama. A few days later, the Montgomery Improvement Association forms and King is elected its president. Parks's arrest sparks a bus boycott that leads to buses being desegregated in that city.

1957 Federal troops are called in to protect nine black students in Little Rock, Arkansas, who are trying to attend all-white Central High School.

1958 King is stabbed with a letter opener at a book signing for *Strive Toward Freedom* in Harlem, New York, on September 20.

1961 President John F. Kennedy issues an executive order prohibiting discrimination in federal hiring on the basis of race, religion, or national origin. The order also establishes the President's Committee on Equal Employment Opportunity, which becomes the EEOC in 1965. Congress on Racial Equality organizes Freedom Rides throughout the South, and the riders suffer beatings from mobs in many cities.

1963 The March on Washington attracts 250,000 people, who listen to Martin Luther King Jr.'s "I Have a Dream" speech.

1964 President Lyndon B. Johnson signs the Civil Rights Act of 1964. King is awarded the Nobel Peace Prize in Oslo, Norway, on December 10.

1965 When an effort to register black voters is met with resistance in the South, Martin Luther King Jr. and the Southern Christian Leadership Council organize a march for voting rights in Alabama from Selma to Montgomery. Congress passes the Voting Rights Act.

1967 Thurgood Marshall becomes the first African-American Supreme Court justice.

1968 Martin Luther King Jr. is assassinated in Memphis, Tennessee on April 4. He is there to support a sanitation workers strike. Later in the year, Coretta Scott King establishes the Martin Luther King, Jr. Center for Nonviolent Social Change in Atlanta.

1986 Martin Luther King Jr. Day is celebrated for the first time as a national holiday in remembrance of King and his message of peaceful protest.

2003 The Supreme Court upholds a University of Michigan Law School policy of using race as a consideration in admitting students.

Glossary

abolitionist An individual who supports that something considered unjust, such as slavery or capital punishment, be ended.

amendment An addition to or expansion of a previously enacted law or document.

apartheid A system of segregation and oppression based on race in South Africa that lasted from 1948 to 1994.

autobiography A person's written account of his or her own life.

Beloved Community A phrase commonly used by Martin Luther King Jr. to describe the ideal community he wished to achieve through nonviolence, based on justice, peace, and harmony.

boycott A form of protest in which a person or group of people intentionally refuses to use a service, purchase goods, or participate in something until changes are instituted.

direct action An act, such as a march or boycott, that aims to effect a specific goal.

injunction A court order that restrains an individual or group from doing a specific activity.

Jim Crow laws A group of laws upheld by state and local governments which supported racial segregation in the South.

legislation A law or group of laws enacted by a government.

militant Having the desire to use force or violence to achieve a goal.

nationalism A desire by a group of people sharing a common history to create a separate and independent nation of their own.

oppression Exercising power with a cruel or unjust purpose.

orator An individual who is a skilled and powerful public speaker.

ordain To officially make someone a religious church minister, pastor, or priest.

pilgrimage A spiritual journey, often to a religious site.

pivotal Describing something of extreme importance that is a turning point.

precedent An action or event that sets a standard and serves as a model for future action.

segregation Keeping people separated based on their race, religion, or other commonalities.

unconstitutional Something that is not in compliance with the system of laws put in place by a city, state, or country.

Further Information

Books

Mortensen, Lori. *Voices of the Civil Rights Movement: A Primary Source Exploration of the Struggle for Racial Equality*. North Mankato, MN: Capstone Press, 2015.

Spilsbury, Richard. *Who Marched for Civil Rights?* Primary Source Detectives. North Mankato, MN: Heinemann-Raintree, 2014.

Staley, Erin. *Martin Luther King Jr. and the Speech that Inspired the World*. A Celebration of the Civil Rights Movement. New York: Rosen Publishing Group, 2015.

Staton, Hilarie. *Civil Rights*. Uncovering the Past: Analyzing Primary Sources. New York: Crabtree Publishing, 2015.

Watson, Stephanie. *Martin Luther King Jr. and the March on Washington*. Stories of the Civil Rights Movement. Edina, MN: ABDO Publishing, 2016.

Websites

Martin Luther King, Jr. Center for Nonviolent Social Change

www.thekingcenter.org

The King Center, located in Atlanta, Georgia, serves as a living memorial to one of the most prolific speakers of the twentieth century and carries on King's message of peaceful protest through nonviolence education. The center also includes a large digital collection of primary sources related to King's life and writings.

The Montgomery Bus Boycott
www.montgomeryboycott.com

The Montgomery Bus Boycott website provides a comprehensive timeline of the bus boycott, its key figures, and interviews with those who peacefully protested. The site also includes a photo gallery, biographies, and headlines from this milestone event in the civil rights movement.

The National Civil Rights Museum
civilrightsmuseum.org

The National Civil Rights Museum is housed at the Lorraine Motel in Memphis, Tennessee, the site of Martin Luther King Jr.'s assassination. Through interactive exhibits, visitors step back in time on a journey from slavery through to the American civil rights movement. The museum also aims to encourage a new generation to stand up and explore current issues, including nonviolence, women's rights, war, riots, poverty, and integration.

Bibliography

Fleming, Alice. *Martin Luther King, Jr.: A Dream of Hope*. New York: Sterling Publishing, 2008.

Jakoubek, Robert. *Martin Luther King, Jr.: Civil Rights Leader*. New York: Chelsea House Publishers, 2005.

———. "Letter from Birmingham Jail." www.thekingcenter.org/archive/document/letter-birmingham-city-jail-0#.

King, Martin Luther, Jr. *A Testament of Hope: The Essential Writings of Martin Luther King, Jr.* Edited by James M. Washington. New York: Harper and Row, 1986.

King Center, The. "Gandhi's Birthday: Dr. King's Tributes to The Mahatma." October 2, 2102. www.thekingcenter.org/news/2012-10-gandhis-birthday-dr-kings-tributes-mahatma.

Lucks, Daniel S. *Selma to Saigon: The Civil Rights Movement and the Vietnam War*. Lexington, KY: University Press of Kentucky, 2014.

Morehouse College. "King at Morehouse." Accessed December 18, 2015. www.morehouse.edu/kingcollection/life.php.

Nobelprize.org. "Acceptance Speech." Delivered December 19, 1964. www.nobelprize.org/nobel_prizes/peace/laureates/1964/king-acceptance_en.html.

NPR. "'Segregation Forever': A Fiery Pledge Forgiven but Not Forgotten." *All Things Considered Radio Diaries*. Last updated January 14, 2013. www.npr.org/2013/01/14/169080969/segregation-forever-a-fiery-pledge-forgiven-but-not-forgotten.

Risen, Clay. "The Passage of the Civil Rights Act." The Gilder Lehrman Institute of American History. Accessed December 18, 2015. www.gilderlehrman.org/history-by-era/civil-rights-movement/essays/passage-civil-rights-act.

Stanford University. "Freedom Rides." Martin Luther King, Jr. and the Global Freedom Struggle. http://kingencyclopedia.stanford.edu/encyclopedia/encyclopedia/enc_freedom_rides.

———. "Montgomery Improvement Association Resolution." Martin Luther King, Jr. and the Global Freedom Struggle. http://kingencyclopedia.stanford.edu/encyclopedia/documentsentry/montgomery_improvement_association_resolution/index.html.

———. "My Pilgrimage to Nonviolence." Martin Luther King, Jr. and the Global Freedom Struggle. http://kingencyclopedia.stanford.edu/encyclopedia/documentsentry/my_pilgrimage_to_nonviolence1.1.html.

———. "Chapter One: Early Years." Martin Luther King, Jr. Research and Education Institute. http://kinginstitute.stanford.edu/king-papers/publications/autobiography-martin-luther-king-jr-contents/chapter-1-early-years.

time.com. "The Assassination." *Time*, January 17, 2002. http://content.time.com/time/magazine/article/0,9171,194842,00.html.

Index

Page numbers in **boldface** are illustrations. Entries in **boldface** are glossary terms.

About the Author

KELLY SPENCE works as a freelance author and editor for educational publishers and holds a BA in English and Liberal Arts from Brock University in St. Catharines, Ontario. When she's not buried in a book, Kelly is busy cooking with her husband or playing with her lovable boxer, Zoey.